Disclaimer

The information contained in this book is for general informational purposes only. While every effort has been made to ensure the accuracy and reliability of the information presented, the author assumes no responsibility for errors or omissions, or for any outcomes related to the use of this information.

Readers are encouraged to verify any information before relying on it. The author is not liable for any losses, injuries, or damages arising from the use of this book.

Acknowledgment

By using this book, you acknowledge that you have read and understood this copyright and disclaimer notice. Thank you for your understanding and support!

Northern Italy......

Welcome to the wonderful realm of Northern Italy, where history, culture, and stunning scenery abound! As you read through the pages of this book, you'll find an area that is as different as it is beautiful—from the magnificent peaks of the Dolomites to the romantic canals of Venice, and from Milan's lively streets to the tranquil beaches of Lake Como.

Northern Italy is more than simply a destination; it's an adventure waiting to happen. Did you know Northern Italy has some of the country's most populated and economically dynamic cities? With over 25 million people, it is home to important towns such as Milan, which is regarded as a worldwide fashion city, and Turin, which is famous for its rich history and exquisite Baroque architecture.

In 2025, visitors can anticipate a vibrant combination of technology and heritage, with continued innovations in sustainable tourism and infrastructural upgrades making it simpler than ever to experience this enchanting area.

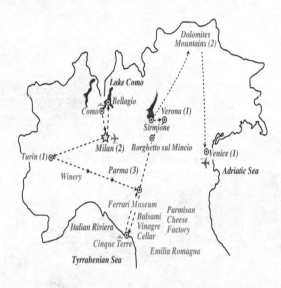

Northern Italy is known for its gorgeous scenery, as well as its lively towns. The area is home to beautiful lakes like Lake Garda and Lake Maggiore, as well as picturesque coastal villages like Cinque Terre. Each site provides a distinct experience, ranging from hiking paths through vineyards to gastronomic trips that highlight local cuisines.

Northern Italy is sometimes referred to as Italy's gourmet heart, where foodies can enjoy anything from delicious risottos to fine wines.

As you plan your trip for 2025, you'll see that Northern Italy is riding a wave of innovation while conserving its rich history. The area has made substantial investments in environmentally friendly transportation choices, with more electric trains and bike-sharing programs cropping up around cities.

Furthermore, many cities are putting in place methods to manage tourism responsibly, ensuring that tourists may enjoy their natural beauty without harming the environment.

However, it is critical to be educated about local legislation. For example, Venice has implemented a minor admission charge during high seasons to regulate visitor numbers and conserve its fragile nature.

These steps demonstrate a growing commitment to responsible tourism, which tourists are increasingly demanding. This guide will help you discover the mysteries of Northern Italy! Inside these pages, you will discover not only useful travel advice but also insider information on hidden jewels that many travelers miss.

We've designed itineraries to suit every style of traveler, whether you're an art fan looking to see world-class institutions or an outdoor enthusiast looking to walk through gorgeous mountain routes.

As you begin on your tour across Northern Italy, we encourage you to thoroughly immerse yourself in the local culture. Enjoy a leisurely supper in a charming trattoria, drink cappuccino while people-watching in a crowded piazza, or get lost in the twisting alleyways of historic villages.

Every second spent here will increase your admiration for this magnificent location. I recall warmly my first vacation to Northern Italy—a spontaneous choice that led me to meander around Verona's cobblestone alleys during golden hour. The warm light of evening lit the historic buildings as I discovered a tiny gelato store and tried my first scoop of pistachio gelato. It was a simple moment, but it captured the charm of this region: surprises around every turn!

Thank you for picking this tour guide for your trip across Northern Italy. Your journey awaits! We invite you to share your experiences by writing an honest evaluation. Your opinion will not only help us develop future editions but will also help other tourists experience the charms of Northern Italy.

So pack your luggage and prepare for an extraordinary experience—Northern Italy is beckoning!

Contents

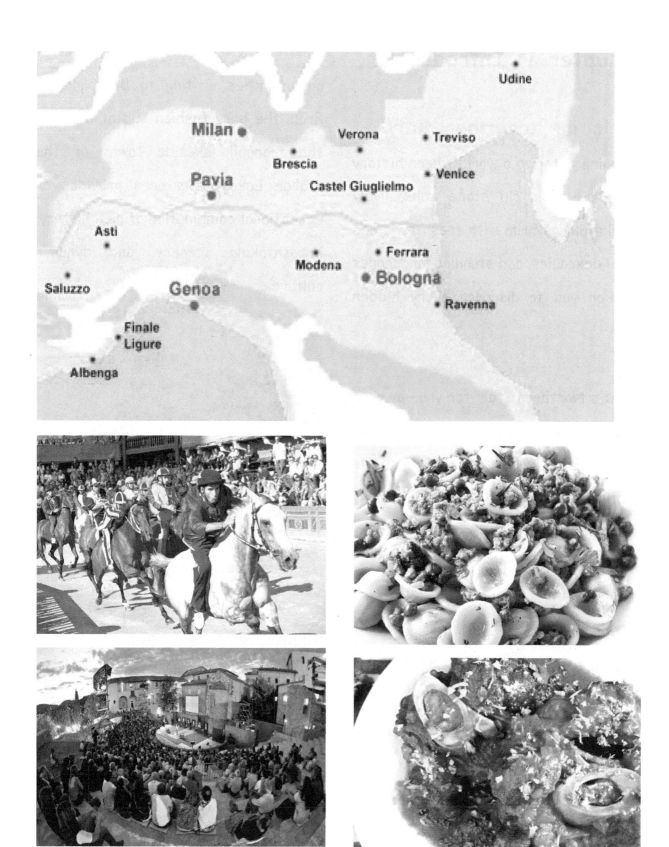

Chapter 1: Introduction.

Welcome to northern Italy.

Imagine entering a world where history whispers from old stone walls, lively marketplaces brim with fresh food and local delicacies, and stunning landscapes beckon you to discover every hidden gem.

That's Northern Italy for you—an area that captures the heart and soul of every visitor who steps foot on its picturesque streets. I vividly recall my first visit to the gorgeous village of Bellagio on Lake Como.

The sun shone on the sea as I wandered down the cobblestone paths, and the seductive perfume of fresh pasta wafted from a neighboring trattoria. It was at that moment, surrounded by such beauty, that I realized Northern Italy was a place I would return to often.

Northern Italy is a treasure mine of opportunities waiting to be explored. From the busy fashion hub of Milan to the tranquil lakeside towns of the Italian Lakes, this area provides an exceptional combination of rich history, breathtaking scenery, and dynamic culture.

The beautiful Alps keep watch to the north, offering a spectacular background for outdoor pursuits all year. Meanwhile, places such as Venice and Bologna provide stunning architecture and gastronomic pleasures to tempt your taste buds.

Statistics show how important Northern Italy is on both a national and international scale. With nearly 25 million people, it is home to some of Italy's greatest cities, such as Milan, Turin, and Verona.

The area accounts for nearly 40% of Italy's GDP, demonstrating its economic vigor. In 2025, guests may expect an even better experience as Northern Italy invests in sustainable tourism initiatives and infrastructural upgrades.

Why Visit Northern Italy Year-Round

One of the most compelling reasons to visit Northern Italy is its capacity to provide unique experiences all year. Each season has its unique appeal and activities to suit everyone's interests, whether you're an adventurer, a cultural buff, or a cuisine aficionado.

Winter Wonderland (December – February)

Winter turns Northern Italy into a beautiful wonderland! The Alps have become a skier's paradise, with world-class destinations such as Cervinia and Val Gardena providing slopes for all ability levels.

Imagine slicing through fresh powder throughout the day and warming up with a drink of mulled wine at a snug mountain chalet in the evening. If skiing isn't your thing, don't miss out on the charming Christmas markets that spring up in places like Bolzano and Milan. Imagine drinking hot chocolate while exploring kiosks selling homemade goods and seasonal treats—there's nothing quite like it!

Spring Awakening (March-May)

As winter fades, spring brings fresh life to Northern Italy's landscapes. This is an excellent season to hike in the Dolomites because wildflowers blossom against the background of towering peaks.

The weather is delightfully moderate, ideal for seeing cities without the summer throngs. You could find yourself walking through Bologna's medieval neighborhoods or taking a leisurely bike ride through the Langhe vineyards while sampling some of Italy's best wines.

Summer Bliss (June-August)

Summer in Northern Italy offers lengthy days of sunlight! Visit the lakes—Lake Garda and Lake Como are ideal for swimming, sailing, or just relaxing on the coast with a good book.

Coastal communities like Cinque Terre come alive with brilliant hues as residents prepare for yearly food and cultural festivals. Don't forget to try gelato at one of the numerous artisanal shops; it's a must!

Autumn Harvest (September-November)

As summer fades into October, Northern Italy's breathtaking foliage emerges—a symphony of reds, oranges, and yellows over vineyards and slopes. This season is especially memorable for foodies since it commemorates truffle hunts in Piedmont and grape harvests across wine regions.

Attend local sagre (food festivals) that celebrate seasonal products, where you may sample anything from freshly squeezed olive oil to exquisite chestnut delicacies.

Northern Italy encourages you to immerse yourself in its rich culture and customs regardless of the season. Whether you're drinking cappuccino at a café in Milan or trekking along gorgeous trails in Trentino-Alto Adige, each encounter will leave you with lifelong memories.

As you experience its charms, we invite you to provide honest feedback via reviews; your insights will help us enhance future editions and benefit other travelers on their journeys.

Chapter 2: Plan Your Northern Italy Adventure

When To Visit: Seasonal Highlights

Northern Italy is a location that shines in every season, with each giving its distinct sensations and charm. Whether you're attracted to the snow-capped summits of the Alps or the sun-kissed beaches of Lake Garda, knowing the seasonal highlights can help you make the most of your trip.

Winter (December through February)

Winter in northern Italy is quite wonderful. The Alps change into a snowy paradise, drawing ski aficionados from all over the world. Cortina d'Ampezzo and Val Gardena provide great skiing conditions, with lift tickets ranging from €50 to €70 per day. If you aren't into skiing, try visiting attractive Christmas markets in locations like Bolzano and Trento, where you can drink mulled wine and eat local specialties like speck and strudel. The weather in the mountains may be cold, with temperatures plunging below freezing, so bring warm clothes!

Spring (March through May)

As winter gives way to spring, Northern Italy explodes with color. This is perhaps one of the finest times to visit, with pleasant weather and fewer visitors. The Dolomites are ideal for trekking this season, with pathways opening up as the snow melts. Daytime temperatures range from 15°C to 20°C (59°F - 68°F), making it perfect for outdoor activities.

Spring also offers a range of local events, such as the renowned Vinitaly wine market in Verona in April, where you can sample some of Italy's greatest wines.

Summer (June–August)

Summer is the busiest tourist season in Northern Italy, particularly in prominent sites such as Venice and Lake Como. Expect warm temperatures of 30°C (86°F) or higher. While this is an excellent season for beach activities along the Italian Riviera or resting by the lake, expect crowds, particularly in July and August, when many Italians holiday as well.

Accommodation prices might skyrocket during this season; reserving ahead of time is critical if you want to get a decent bargain. Look for local summer events that celebrate everything from cuisine to music!

Autumn (September through November)

Autumn is an excellent time to explore Northern Italy. The weather continues nicely, with average temperatures of approximately 20°C (68°F) in September and progressively decreasing by November.

This season is famed for its harvest celebrations; in October, you may go truffle hunting in Alba or pick grapes in Tuscany's vineyards. The autumn foliage lends another element of grandeur to the landscapes—imagine wandering through vineyards with vines flaming in colors of crimson and gold!

Budgeting for Your Trip

Budgeting for your vacation to Northern Italy may be as simple or complex as you like! It's all about understanding what to anticipate and preparing properly.

Accommodation Costs:

Accommodation rates vary greatly according to location and kind. In big cities like Milan and Venice, mid-range hotels cost between €100 and €250 a night on average. Charming bed and breakfasts or agriturismos may be found in smaller towns or rural locations for €70-€120 per night. Hostels for budget tourists normally cost between €40 and €60 per night. Dining expenses

Dining out might also differ significantly **depending on your choices:**

- **Cheap Eats:** Grab-and-go meals, such as pizza slices or paninis, may cost between €5 and €10.

- **Mid-range Restaurants:** A sit-down dinner normally costs €20-€35 per person.

- **Fine Dining:** For a more upmarket experience, budget €50 or more per person.

To save money while having real experiences, eat where locals do—look for locations that are off the main path and do not cater largely to visitors.

Transportation Costs

Getting around Northern Italy is relatively reasonable if you plan carefully.

- **Trains:** The rail system is reliable and links most major cities. Tickets vary from €5 to €25, depending on distance and class. Book early to save money!

- **Buses:** Companies such as Flixbus provide cost-effective solutions, with rates ranging from €10 to €30.

- **Car Rentals:** If you want flexibility, hiring a car costs between €30 and €60 per day, including gasoline. Remember that parking fines may add up quickly, particularly in city centers.

Daily Budget Overview

Plan a daily budget of €75-€150 per person, which covers lodging, food, transportation, and **activities. Here is a basic breakdown:**

- Accommodation costs €70 (average for budget tourists).
- Meals: €50 (a combination of inexpensive nibbles and one sit-down supper).
- Transportation: €15 (local bus or a short rail journey).
- Activities cost €20 (admission fees or guided excursions).

By keeping an eye on your expenditures and choosing local experiences over tourist traps, you can enjoy everything that Northern Italy has to offer without breaking the bank!

Getting Around Northern Italy.

Northern Italy's well-connected transportation network makes it relatively simple to navigate. Here's everything you need to know about **getting around:**

Trains

Italy's rail system is one of the greatest in Europe! High-speed trains, like the Frecciarossa, link major cities like Milan, Venice, Florence, and Bologna swiftly and pleasantly. For example:

- Milan to Venice takes around 2 hours; tickets vary from €25 to €60.
- Venice to Florence takes around 2 hours; fares start at about €20.
- To get the cheapest discounts, book your tickets ahead of time using platforms such as Trainline or Trenitalia.

Buses

- Buses are an excellent choice for places that are difficult to reach by rail or if you want to save money.
- Flixbus provides various routes across Northern Italy, with tickets ranging from €10 to €30 depending on distance.

Car Rentals

If you want to explore rural regions or smaller towns at your leisure, renting a vehicle can be the ideal option! Rental fees typically start at about €30 per day but may rise depending on demand and car type.

Simply bear in mind that driving in cities might be difficult owing to small streets and limited parking alternatives.

Public Transportation Within Cities

Most cities have reliable public transit networks, which include buses, trams, and metro lines.

- **Milan**: The metro system serves significant regions; single tickets cost around €2.
- Venice's unique layout without vehicles makes walking the ideal way to explore! Vaporetto (water bus) prices begin at €7.50 for a single journey.

Insider Tips

- **Book Early**: Train costs might change depending on demand; buying beforehand frequently results in lower pricing.

- **Travel Off-Peak**: If possible, avoid traveling on big holidays or weekends, when costs tend to rise.

- **Use Public Transportation:** It is not only inexpensive, but it also enables you to experience local life while traveling.

With these tips on when to visit Northern Italy, how to pay for your trip, and how to navigate its transportation choices, you'll be well on your way to planning an incredible journey! Enjoy every minute as you visit this gorgeous area rich in history, culture, and breathtaking scenery!

Chapter 3: Top Destinations in Northern Italy

Milan

Milan, the bustling capital of Lombardy, is a city that seamlessly blends its deep historical origins with cutting-edge technology. As you walk through the lively streets, you can sense the pulse of creativity and invention that runs through this city.

I remember well my first evening in Milan—after a day of traveling, I found myself on Duomo's rooftop balcony, watching the sunset paint the sky in shades of orange and pink over the city. It was a moment of pure enchantment that captured the spirit of Milan: a city where history and modern life live together.

History & Architecture

Milan's history extends back to Roman times when it was known as Mediolanum, a major colony in the Roman Empire. The city's advantageous position established it as a commercial and cultural center, laying the basis for its eventual importance. Fast forward to the Middle Ages, when Milan grew into a strong city-state ruled by important dynasties such as the Visconti and Sforza.

One cannot visit Milan without admiring its architectural treasures. The Duomo di Milano, or Milan Cathedral, is a magnificent specimen of Gothic architecture that took over six centuries to construct! Its ornate façade includes over 3,400 sculptures, 135 spires, and a stunning rooftop with panoramic views of the city.

Make sure to ascend to the top (tickets cost between €10 and €15) for a spectacular experience. Another historical site is Sforza Castle (Castello Sforzesco), which was erected as a stronghold by Francesco Sforza in the 15th century. This massive edifice today houses many museums and art collections, including masterpieces by Michelangelo and Leonardo da Vinci. The castle grounds are ideal for a leisurely walk, where you can absorb both history and beauty.

Milan's architectural environment also has beautiful specimens of the Renaissance and Baroque periods.

The Galleria Vittorio Emanuele II, only steps from the Duomo, is one of the world's oldest retail malls, with a stunning glass dome and beautiful mosaics. It is more than simply a shopping mall; it is a cultural monument where you may appreciate architecture and premium products.

Fashion & Design

Milan is generally regarded as the world's fashion capital—and with good cause! The city is home to some of the most prominent fashion brands, including Prada, Gucci, and Versace. The Quadrilatero della Moda, or Fashion District, is home to high-end stores on streets such as Via Montenapoleone and Via della Spiga.

Even if you're not looking for luxury clothing, going through this area is an experience in and of itself; it's like walking through an open-air museum of fashion. Every year, Milan holds Milan Fashion Week, which is one of the most anticipated events on the worldwide fashion calendar. This week-long festival features cutting-edge designs from both renowned businesses and young talent.

Even if you don't get an invitation to a runway show, there are plenty of other events going on across the city, including exhibits, parties, and pop-up stores that celebrate fashion in all its manifestations.

Aside from Fashion Week, Milan has several design events, including the Salone del Mobile, which takes place in April. This international furniture expo brings together designers from all over the world to display their creative furniture and interior design ideas. It is a must-see for everyone interested in design!

Dinner and Nightlife

After taking up all of the culture and history, it's time to indulge in Milan's gastronomic pleasures! The city has a remarkable selection of culinary alternatives that appeal to every taste. For true Milanese food, try risotto alla Milanese, a creamy saffron-infused rice dish that is truly divine—go to Trattoria Milanese.

For those looking for something more informal yet wonderful, visit Mercato Centrale near Milano Centrale train station. This colorful food market has kiosks from local merchants selling anything from fresh pasta to artisanal cheeses—ideal for trying out local tastes or grabbing a fast snack.

As night falls, Milan's nightlife comes to life! The Navigli region is well-known for its scenic canals lined with cafés and restaurants, making it perfect for sipping an aperitivo (pre-dinner drink) while watching inhabitants go about their evening activities. As you mix with other visitors and locals, try the Spritz, a delicious beverage prepared with Prosecco and Aperol.

For those seeking for something more expensive, Terrazza Aperol, situated directly by the Duomo, offers spectacular views of the Piazza del Duomo and is ideal for sipping drinks while taking in the scenery. Whether you're seeing historical buildings during the day or having fun at night with music and laughter, Milan guarantees a memorable experience full of elegance, creativity, and rich culture. So prepare to immerse into this dynamic city—it awaits you with open arms!

The Dolomites

The Dolomites, a UNESCO World Heritage site, are a stunning mountain range in northern Italy that attracts both adventurers and nature enthusiasts.

These mountains, with their spectacular peaks, verdant valleys, and crystal-clear lakes, provide an excellent background for a wide range of outdoor activities. I recall my first trip to this magnificent region: the air was crisp, the sun was shining, and as I approached a viewpoint overlooking the famed Tre Cime di Lavaredo, I had an overpowering feeling of tranquility and connection to nature. The Dolomites are genuinely a location where you can get away from the hustle and bustle of daily life and immerse yourself in the majesty of nature.

Hiking and Outdoor Activities.

Summer is the best time to hike in the Dolomites, with paths ranging from pleasant strolls to strenuous excursions that reward you with breathtaking vistas. Here are a few **must-do hikes:**

Tre Cime di Lavaredo Circuit

- **Distance**: 8.8 kilometers (5.5 miles).

The difficulty is moderate.

- **Altitude Change**: 425 meters (1,400 feet)
- **Trailhead**: Rifugio Auronzo Parking Lot

This renowned climb takes you around the three towering peaks known as the Tre Cime. The trek begins at the Rifugio Auronzo and provides

breathtaking views of the surrounding terrain. It is well-marked.

During the summer, wildflowers may be seen covering the meadows. While it might be crowded, particularly in August, the stunning beauty is well worth the trip.

Lago di Sorapis

- **Distance**: 11.6 kilometers (7.2 miles).
- **Difficulty**: Moderate to Hard
- **Altitude Change**: 460 meters (1,520 feet)
- **Trailhead**: Near the Passo Tre Croci.

This trek takes you to one of the most stunning lakes in the Dolomites, famed for its vibrant blue hue. The trek may be difficult at times, with tiny trails and steep slopes, so only those who are comfortable with heights should attempt it. The views from the lake are breathtaking—ideal for a picnic.

Cinque Torri.

- **Distance**: 1.9 kilometers (1.2 miles) circle
- **Difficulty**: Easy
- **Total Ascent**: 130 meters (430 feet)
- **Location**: Near Cortina d'Ampezzo.

This short but attractive loop around five unique rock towers that are popular among climbers. Along the journey, you'll come across World War I remains such as trenches and bunkers, making this trip both attractive and historically important.

Lago di Braies

- **Distance**: 3.7 kilometers (2.3 miles) circle
- **Difficulty**: Easy
- **Total ascent:** little.

This lovely lake is known for its breathtaking blue waters surrounded by high hills. The level walk around the lake is ideal for families, with lots of opportunities for photography or quiet moments by the water. In addition to hiking, summer in the Dolomites is perfect for mountain biking, rock climbing, and even paragliding! Many paths are suited to cyclists, enabling you to explore more secluded locations while experiencing thrilling descents.

Skiing and Winter Sport

When the Dolomites are blanketed with snow, they become a winter sports paradise.

- **Ski Resorts:** The Dolomiti Superski region has about 1,200 kilometers (745 miles) of slopes spread over many resorts. Some prominent ski locations are:

- **Cortina d'Ampezzo:** Known as the "Queen of the Dolomites," this resort has a variety of skiing slopes for all ability levels and breathtaking vistas.

- **Val Gardena** is well-known for its well-kept slopes and stunning landscape, making it ideal for both beginners and expert skiers.

- **Marmolada:** With the highest mountain in the Dolomites, Marmolada provides demanding routes and beautiful glacier vistas.

Ski passes normally cost between €50 and €70 per day, depending on the resort and time of year; multi-day tickets might save you a lot of money if you intend on staying for a while.

Aside from skiing, there are plenty of other winter activities:

- **Snowshoeing:** With snowshoes, you may explore tranquil routes through snowy woods; many rental businesses provide guided trips.

- **Cross-Country Skiing:** With so many paths accessible, this is an excellent opportunity to appreciate winter scenery at a leisurely pace.

- **Ice Climbing:** For adrenaline seekers, ice climbing classes are offered, where you can learn to conquer frozen waterfalls with professional assistance.

Charming Mountain Towns.

The Dolomites are filled with lovely villages, each offering its own distinct culture and **experiences**:

- **Cortina d'Ampezzo**: Known as Italy's best ski resort town, Cortina mixes elegance and magnificent landscape. Stroll through its pedestrian-friendly streets, which are dotted with upscale stores and comfortable cafés. Don't miss out on eating local delicacies such as speck (cured ham) or strudel at one of the numerous eateries.

- **Ortisei**: Located in Val Gardena, Ortisei is known for its wood carving history and breathtaking mountain surroundings. The village has a welcoming ambiance, with colorful houses that resemble Tyrolean architecture. Visit during summer or winter festivals to see local customs directly, such as folk music performances or traditional crafts.

- **Alba di Canazei**: During the summer, this small community serves as a gateway to some of the area's greatest hiking routes, while in the winter, it turns into a skiing center. Its lovely lanes are lined with stores offering homemade crafts and local delicacies—ideal for picking up keepsakes!

As you tour these places, take the time to talk with the inhabitants; their anecdotes about living in this beautiful area will greatly improve your experience. The Dolomites provide more than simply outdoor experiences; they also provide opportunities to interact with nature and immerse oneself in local culture. Whether you're hiking under the bright sky or skiing down pristine slopes, every minute you spend here will leave you with lifelong memories!

Venice

Venice, the lovely "Floating City," is unlike any other. When you get off the train at Santa Lucia station and receive your first view of the Grand Canal, you'll be taken aback by the city's ageless splendor. The sight of gondolas drifting down the famed rivers, the sound of laughter and conversation flowing out of quaint cafés, and the perfume of freshly baked focaccia wafting through the air—it's a sensory feast that will capture you completely.

Notable Canals and Gondola Rides

Venice's canals are the city's lifeblood, acting as roadways, highways, and meeting spaces for both residents and tourists. The Grand Canal, Venice's major thoroughfare, is a must-see, reaching over 3.8 kilometers (2.4 miles) and flowing through the city. As you travel down its serpentine road, you'll be treated to a breathtaking exhibition of Venetian architecture, ranging from the Gothic grandeur of the Ca' d'Oro to the Renaissance elegance of the Palazzo Contarini del Bovolo.

However, the genuine Venetian experience is a trip in a classic gondola. These distinctive flat-bottomed boats have been cruising Venice's waterways for centuries, and a 30-minute trip is an excellent opportunity to see the city's secret canals and lanes.

As your expert gondolier guides you over the water with a single oar, you'll feel transported back in time, surrounded by the city's timeless splendor. Many gondola stations provide the option of adding a serenade to your trip, which includes a live soundtrack provided by a singer or guitarist.

Saint Mark's Square and Basilica

A vacation to Venice is not complete without a stop at St. Mark's area (Piazza San Marco), the city's major public area, and a hive of activity. The plaza is dominated by the beautiful St. Mark's Basilica, a Byzantine architectural marvel with shimmering golden mosaics and complex marble flooring. Construction of the basilica started in the eleventh century, and it has functioned as Venice's cathedral for more than 800 years.

To avoid crowds, try to arrive early in the morning or late in the day. If you wish to enter the basilica, dress correctly (no shorts or sleeveless shirts are permitted) and be prepared to wait in line. The area also houses the Doge's Palace, the historic seat of Venice's rulers, which is well worth a visit for its sumptuous furnishings and rich history.

Explore the Floating City

While the major attractions in Venice are undeniably magnificent, some of the city's most pleasant and unforgettable encounters may be discovered off the beaten route.

Take a short boat journey to the surrounding islands of Murano and Burano, which are renowned for their traditional crafts. Murano is well-known for its glassblowing, and visitors may see talented artists produce beautiful pieces of art at one of the island's numerous glass factories. Burano, on the other hand, is noted for its colorful buildings and beautiful lace, which can be seen being created by local women at the island's lace museum.

Another excellent approach to experiencing Venice is to get lost in the city's twisting passageways and canals. Discover secret churches like the Basilica of Santa Maria della Salute, which has a magnificent white marble exterior, or small bacari (wine bars) that serve cicchetti (Venetian tapas) and local wine.

Don't forget to try some of Venice's famed cuisine, which ranges from fresh seafood dishes like spaghetti alle vongole (spaghetti with clams) to sweet sweets like the iconic tiramisu.

Venice is a city that grabs the hearts and imaginations of all visitors. Whether you're admiring the grandeur of St. Mark's Basilica, skimming around the canals in a gondola, or just taking in the city's distinct ambiance, you'll leave with memories to last a lifetime. So, embrace your inner adventurer and prepare to uncover the enchantment of Venice!

Bologna

Bologna, the capital of Emilia-Romagna, is sometimes referred to as Italy's gastronomic capital, a label it proudly wears. As I walked through its meandering alleyways for the first time, I was impressed by the dynamic atmosphere—aromas of boiling sauces and freshly baked bread wafting from trattorias, as well as the boisterous talk of people enjoying their dinners outside.

Bologna is a city that encourages you to enjoy not only its cuisine but also its rich history and culture.

Bologna is famous for its gourmet scene, and rightly so! The city's hearty and rich gastronomic offerings have earned it the endearing moniker "La Grassa," which means "The Fat One."

Tagliatelle al ragù, often known as spaghetti Bolognese outside of Italy, is central to Bologna's culinary traditions. This meal consists of thin, ribbon-like spaghetti served with a very fragrant and complex slow-cooked meat sauce prepared from beef, pork, tomatoes, onions, and a splash of red wine.

This meal is available at practically every trattoria in the city, but for a genuine experience, go to Trattoria Anna Maria, where the pasta is prepared fresh every day.

Tortellini, a little stuffed pasta loaded with meat and cheese, is another local favorite. It's often served in a thick broth (tortellini in brodo), which warms the spirit on cold days.

Osteria dell'Orsa serves the greatest tortellini in town, and you can see the cooks create this renowned delicacy right in front of you.

Bologna is particularly known for its mortadella, a delectable cured pig sausage with little chunks of fat that give it a distinct taste and texture. It's often served sliced thin on crusty bread or as part of an antipasto dish. Tamburini, a classic deli that has served residents since 1932, offers some of the best mortadella.

To immerse yourself in Bologna's food culture, visit Mercato di Mezzo, a lively market in the Quadrilatero neighborhood. Here, you'll discover a variety of fresh fruit, cheeses, meats, and local specialties. It's the ideal spot to grab a snack or get some items to take home.

Historical University Town

Bologna is not only about cuisine; it is also home to one of the world's oldest institutions, the University of Bologna, which was established in 1088. This prominent school has defined the city's character for centuries and continues to draw students from across the world today.

As you travel through the university area, you will witness exquisite medieval architecture mixed with contemporary structures housing several institutions.

The university's ancient campus includes breathtaking structures such as the Archiginnasio, which was formerly the university's main building but today contains the interesting Anatomical Theatre—an elegant auditorium where anatomy lectures were previously taught.

The presence of students lends liveliness to Bologna's ambiance; bustling cafés are packed with young people discussing their studies over espresso or enjoying an aperitivo in the early evening. The student community here contributes greatly to Bologna's cultural scene—look for art exhibits, music festivals, and theatrical performances all year.

Porticoes & Towers

One of Bologna's most distinguishing characteristics is its porticoes, a network of covered walkways that spans 38 kilometers (about 24 miles) throughout the city. These porticoes not only give protection from the rain and sun but also add to Bologna's distinct architectural appeal, setting it apart from other Italian towns.

The most renowned portico goes up to the San Luca Sanctuary on Colle della Guardia hill, providing a picturesque stroll with breathtaking views of Bologna as you climb its 666 arches—a meaningful number! This unhurried journey is especially magnificent at sunset when the city shines with golden colors.

Bologna is also recognized for its distinctive towers, including the Asinelli Tower and its lesser cousin, the Garisenda Tower. Climbing the Asinelli Tower, which stands at 97 meters (318 feet), is a rite of passage for tourists looking for panoramic views of the city.

The ascent consists of 498 steps, but once at the summit, you're rewarded with stunning views of Bologna's terracotta roofs. The towers date back to the Middle Ages when affluent families constructed them as emblems of power and rank, as well as watchtowers to protect against invasions. Today, they serve as historical sites, telling tales about Bologna's history.

To summarize, Bologna is a city rich in gastronomic pleasures, intellectual tradition, and distinctive architecture that invites visitors to discover its hidden jewels. Whether you're indulging in local delicacies or meandering through historic alleys dotted with porticoes and turrets, you'll immediately understand why Bologna is so precious to Italians. So, take your fork and spirit of adventure—Bologna awaits!

Florence

Florence, the birthplace of the Renaissance, is a city brimming with art, history, and culture around every corner. When I first arrived in Florence, I was fascinated by the bustling streets packed with artists and performers, as well as the seductive scent of freshly prepared Italian food floating through the air.

As I stood in front of the beautiful Duomo, with the light throwing a golden color on its ornate façade, I felt as if I had entered a live painting. Florence is more than simply a place; it's an experience that wakes the senses and piques the imagination.

Renaissance Art and Architecture

Florence is home to some of the most important works of Renaissance art and architecture. The Uffizi Gallery is a must-see for art lovers. This world-renowned museum has an outstanding collection of works by artists like Botticelli, Michelangelo, and Leonardo da Vinci. Be sure to look for Botticelli's The Birth of Venus, a breathtaking depiction of beauty and love that has captivated audiences for ages.

The Uffizi also houses Michelangelo's Doni Tondo, the artist's only circle painting to stay in Florence.

Florence's architecture is similarly impressive. The Florence Cathedral (Santa Maria del Fiore) is the city's defining emblem, with its majestic dome designed by Filippo Brunelleschi and finished in 1436.

The cathedral's façade is decorated with multicolored marble in tones of green, pink, and white, producing a magnificent visual impression. Inside, stunning paintings and sculptures depict tales of faith and craftsmanship.

Another architectural marvel is Piazza della Signoria, the city's political core. You may view the majestic Palazzo Vecchio, which has remained since the 14th century and is currently used as Florence's municipal hall.

The area also has a copy of Michelangelo's David, which stands proudly outside the Palazzo, while the real can be seen at the neighboring Accademia Gallery.

Dome and Ponte Vecchio

The Duomo is more than simply an architectural beauty; it also has historical and cultural importance for the Florentines. The Opera di Santa Maria del Fiore commissioned its construction, which started in 1296 on the site of an ancient church dedicated to Santa Reparata.

The cathedral was intended to be larger than any other church in Europe at the time, symbolizing Florence's riches and influence during the Renaissance. The dome itself was innovative; Brunelleschi designed a self-supporting structure that allowed for its immense size without the need for scaffolding—a breakthrough feat for the time. Climbing to the top of the dome offers breathtaking panoramic views of Florence.

One of Florence's most iconic sites, the Ponte Vecchio, is just a short walk from the Duomo. This ancient bridge crosses the Arno River and is surrounded by stores selling goldsmith's products and handmade crafts, a practice that dates back to when butchers held these locations. Today, it's a gorgeous location ideal for taking great images at sunset as the golden light reflects off the sea.

Tuscan Cuisine and Wine.

No trip to Florence is complete without indulging in its gastronomic pleasures! Tuscan food is characterized by its simplicity and use of fresh ingredients.

One must-try delicacy is Bistecca alla Fiorentina, a thick T-bone steak seasoned with salt and cooked over an open flame until perfectly charred on the exterior but juicy on the inside—best served with a glass of Chianti wine.

Another local favorite is Pici cacio e pepe, which is handmade pasta mixed with pecorino cheese and black pepper—a great comfort dish that perfectly reflects Tuscan characteristics. For dessert, try cantucci, which are crunchy almond pastries often paired with Vin Santo, a sweet dessert wine ideal for dipping.

To properly experience Tuscan wine, plan a day excursion to adjacent vineyards in Chianti or Montalcino. Many vineyards have tours where you may learn about traditional winemaking techniques while tasting delicious wines combined with local cheeses and cured foods.

A visit to Castello di Verrazzano or Antinori nel Chianti Classico will deliver not only wonderful tastes but also breathtaking vistas of rolling vineyards.

Florence is more than simply a city; it is a celebration of art, history, and cuisine, inviting you to discover its hidden gems at every step. Whether you're admiring Renaissance masterpieces at world-class museums or enjoying wonderful foods coupled with superb wines, every minute spent here will make an unforgettable impression on your heart—just like it did on mine! So bring your camera, hunger, and sense of wonder—Florence awaits!

Cinque Terre.

Cinque Terre, which translates to "Five Lands," is a breathtaking coastal area on the Ligurian Sea known for its charming towns, spectacular cliffs, and lively scenery.

When I first arrived in this gorgeous place via train, the sight of colorful cottages clinging to steep slopes against the background of turquoise seas stole my breath away. It seemed like walking into a postcard, with each community having its distinct charm and personality ready to be discovered.

Colorful Fishing Villages.

Cinque Terre consists of five picturesque villages: Monterosso al Mare, Vernazza, Corniglia, Manarola, and Riomaggiore. Every community has its unique charm and attractions.

Monterosso al Mare: The biggest of the five, Monterosso is known for its lovely sandy beaches, which make it a favorite destination for sunbathers and swimmers. The village has a picturesque old town with narrow lanes filled with stores offering local products and wonderful gelato. Don't miss out on seeing the Church of San Giovanni Battista, which originates from the 12th century and has exquisite Gothic architecture.

Vernazza: Often regarded as the most gorgeous of the settlements, Vernazza is distinguished by its colorful buildings piled on top of one another and its lovely port filled with fishing boats.

The settlement is home to the Doria Castle, which provides panoramic views of the coastline. Walking through its small lanes, you'll come across charming eateries selling fresh seafood and locally sourced wines.

Corniglia, perched high on a cliff, is unusual in that it does not have direct access to the sea. To get there, ascend roughly 382 stairs from the train station! This exertion is rewarded with stunning views of the vineyards and beach. Corniglia is famed for its native white wine, Sciacchetrà, which may be sampled in one of the village's wine bars.

Manarola is one of Cinque Terre's oldest communities and is well-known for its charming appeal. Its brightly colored houses are positioned against high cliffs, providing an attractive scene.

The community is well-known for its Via dell'Amore, a picturesque walking route that links it to Riomaggiore. Make sure to visit the nearby vineyards and drink wines produced from grapes cultivated on terraced slopes.

- **Riomaggiore**: Riomaggiore, the southernmost settlement, has a gorgeous waterfront and colorful homes that seem to slide down into the sea. The village's main thoroughfare, Via Colombo, is lined with stores and restaurants serving local cuisine. The Church of San Giovanni Battista, built in the 14th century, is a must-see.

Throughout the year, each town celebrates its unique customs and festivals, which range from cuisine to music. Interacting with locals at these events can help you appreciate their culture and way of life.

Hiking on Coastal Trails

Hiking along the magnificent coastal pathways that link the villages is one of the greatest ways to explore Cinque Terre. Here are a few common **routes**:

Sentiero Azzurro (Blue route): This renowned route connects all five communities and provides breathtaking views of the ocean. The route from Monterosso to Vernazza is about 3.5 km (2 miles) long and takes around 1.5 hours to trek; it is rated moderately challenging owing to some steep parts, but hikers are rewarded with beautiful views along the way.

Vernazza to Corniglia: This leg is significantly longer, measuring about 3 kilometers (1.9 miles) and taking around 1 hour to complete. It offers stunning vistas of terraced vineyards and rocks that plunge into the sea.

Manarola to Riomaggiore (Via dell'Amore): This simple, level route runs for around 1 kilometer (0.6 miles) along the cliffs overlooking the sea and takes about 20 minutes to walk. While it has been closed for refurbishment in recent years, local reports indicate that it has reopened periodically.

- **Safety Considerations**: Always verify trail conditions before leaving, since certain pathways may be blocked due to landslides or inclement weather. Wear solid hiking shoes, bring water, and don't forget your camera—the vistas are just stunning!

Seafood and local wines.

Cinque Terre's coastline setting ensures that fresh seafood is important to its gastronomic **offerings. Here are some foods you must try:**

Anchovies, also known as acciughe in Cinque Terre, are a common ingredient in numerous meals, whether fried, marinated in lemon juice, or packed into savory pastries.

Muscoli Ripieni (filled Mussels): A delightful meal created with fresh mussels filled with breadcrumbs, herbs, and spices, which pairs well with a bottle of local wine.

Trofie al Pesto: This typical Ligurian pasta meal consists of twisted spaghetti served with fresh basil pesto created from local ingredients such as pine nuts and Parmigiano-Reggiano.

Cinque Terre produces several amazing sorts of wine due to its distinctive terraced vines facing the sea.

Cinque Terre DOC: This dry white wine is manufactured mostly from native grape varietals, including Bosco, Albarola, and Vermentino. Its sharp taste profile works well with seafood recipes.

Sciacchetrà is a sweet dessert wine created from partly dried grapes painstakingly collected from steep hillsides. It has rich notes of honey and almonds—a wonderful pleasure!

To improve your gastronomic experience, try taking a wine-tasting trip at one of the local vineyards, where you can drink these excellent wines combined with traditional foods and learn about their production processes from dedicated winemakers. Cinque Terre is more than simply a location; it's a journey full of bright hues, rich cuisines, and amazing experiences waiting to be discovered! So tie up your walking shoes, bring your hunger for wonderful food and wine, and get ready for an unforgettable adventure through these charming seaside towns!

Genoa

Genoa, the bustling capital of Liguria, is rich in marine history and culture. When I first walked through its labyrinthine alleyways, I was captivated by the colorful atmosphere—the aroma of fresh seafood mixed with the salty sea wind, and the sounds of laughing bounced off old stone walls.

This city, with its rich history and gorgeous architecture, is like a living museum waiting to be discovered.

Europe's Largest Historical City Center

Genoa is one of the biggest old city cores in Europe, spanning an amazing 113 hectares. This UNESCO World Heritage-listed region is a labyrinth of small passageways known as caruggi, where you may easily get lost and uncover hidden jewels around every corner.

The old town is a reminder of Genoa's maritime heritage, with magnificent palaces and cathedrals that represent the city's previous splendor as a great maritime republic.

As you meander through these twisting lanes, you'll come across Piazza De Ferrari, the city's main plaza, which acts as a hive of activity and an excellent starting place for your journey. Dominated by the imposing Palazzo Ducale, this piazza is surrounded by spectacular architecture that offers tales about the city's rich history.

Don't miss the Cathedral of San Lorenzo, which was erected in the 12th century on the foundation of an older church. Its bold black-and-white striped front and ornate interior are stunning. Inside, visitors may discover the relics of Genoa's patron saint, St. John the Baptist—a must-see for anybody interested in the city's religious history.

As you go farther into the ancient center, you'll come across Via Garibaldi, also known as Strada Nuova, which is flanked by majestic palaces that were formerly home to aristocratic families. Many of these structures are now museums that house magnificent art collections, including masterpieces by Caravaggio and Rubens.

The architectural styles here vary from Renaissance to Baroque, providing a visual feast for history buffs. The essence of Genoa lives in these lanes, where fragrances from local food stores (sciamadde) fill the air and centuries-old traditions are revived in artisan workshops.

Keep a look out for botteghe storiche (historic stores) that have been serving the community for centuries; they are a tribute to the city's ongoing workmanship.

Aquarium and Marine History

The Aquarium of Genoa, one of Europe's biggest aquariums, celebrates Genoa's nautical history and is a must-see destination for both families and marine aficionados.

This aquarium, located in the restored Old Port district and constructed by famous architect Renzo Piano, houses around 15,000 creatures representing hundreds of species from varied environments across the globe.

As you tour its spectacular displays, you'll see everything from playful dolphins to fascinating jellyfish. The aquarium also has interactive exhibits that teach visitors about marine conservation and the necessity of maintaining our seas.

The Museum of the Sea is next to the aquarium and offers a closer look into Genoa's rich nautical history. Discover intriguing items from old ships, navigational tools used by explorers, and displays highlighting Genoa's position as a significant commercial port throughout history.

A trip around Genoa's Old Port reveals more about the city's nautical history; keep an eye out for historic ships docked nearby and enjoy riverfront cuisine with harbor views.

Pesto with Focaccia

Not only does Genoa have gorgeous architecture and a rich history, but it is also a gourmet heaven! Pesto alla Genovese, a fragrant sauce prepared from fresh basil, garlic, pine nuts, Parmesan cheese, and olive oil, originated in this city. This brilliant green sauce is generally served over trofie or trenette pasta and is a must-try meal when here.

For a real pesto experience, visit Pasta Fresca or Da Maria, where you can have handmade pasta mixed with freshly prepared pesto that will take your taste buds to Liguria.

Another local delicacy is focaccia, a delectable flatbread that comes in a variety of flavors and is often topped with olive oil, rosemary, or olives. Antica Friggitoria and Focacceria di San Francesco both provide delicious focaccia and have been popular among locals for years.

To properly experience Genoese cuisine, try taking a culinary tour that takes you around local markets and cafés, where you may taste these delicacies while learning about their origins from knowledgeable locals.

Finally, Genoa is a city that seamlessly mixes its rich maritime heritage, lively culture, and gastronomic brilliance. Whether you're touring its ancient center, which is replete with architectural masterpieces, or eating genuine cuisine like pesto and focaccia at delightful restaurants, every minute spent here will amaze you with its charm. So take your camera and your appetite—Genoa is waiting!

Turin

Turin, the exquisite capital of the Piedmont region, is sometimes eclipsed by more renowned Italian cities such as Rome and Florence, but it has a certain appeal all its own.

As I walked through the city for the first time, I was intrigued by its broad boulevards, gorgeous baroque architecture, and rich history. The scent of freshly made coffee drifting from surrounding cafés tempted me to pause and enjoy this wonderful city.

Turin is a city where history and modernity collide, making it an ideal destination for tourists looking for an authentic Italian experience.

Royal Residences & Baroque Architecture

Turin is well-known for its royal mansions, which represent the city's historic prominence as the seat of the House of Savoy. The Palazzo Reale

(Royal Palace) is a superb example of Baroque architecture and a symbol of the city's royal heritage.

Originally erected in the 16th century, this palace had multiple restorations, resulting in rich rooms adorned with murals, symphonies, and exquisite furniture.

When you enter, be sure to check out the Royal Apartments, where you can see sumptuous rooms like the Hall of Mirrors and the Royal Chapel, which are decorated with complex details and stunning artwork. The palace also has enormous gardens known as the Giardini Reali, which are ideal for a leisurely walk around fountains and groomed hedges.

Another must-see attraction is the Palazzo Madama, which stands boldly in Piazza Castello. This ancient palace, which houses the Museum of Ancient Art, blends aspects of medieval and baroque architecture. You may examine a wide collection of items from the Roman period to the Renaissance.

Don't miss the Basilica di Superga, which sits on a hill overlooking Turin. This majestic chapel was erected to commemorate Victor Amadeus II triumph against the French in 1706 and provides amazing views of the city below. The basilica's interior is similarly magnificent, with stunning murals and an exquisite altar.

Egyptian Museum & Contemporary Art

One of Turin's most impressive attractions is the Museo Egizio (Egyptian Museum), which displays one of the most significant collections of ancient Egyptian antiquities outside of Cairo.

This museum, founded in 1824, has about 30,000 items of ancient Egyptian art, including mummies, sarcophagi, sculptures, and daily artifacts.

As you approach the museum, you'll be met with stunning exhibits that chronologically depict Egyptian civilization from its inception to its later centuries. The Tomb of Kha will surely be the highlight of your tour since it includes not only funerary goods but also food offerings that provide light on ancient burial rituals.

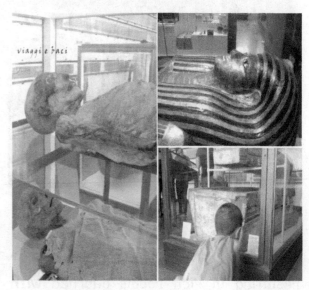

The museum has undergone major renovations to improve the tourist experience, including contemporary lighting and interactive displays that bring history to life. Check out noteworthy treasures such as Ramesses II's sitting statue and wonderfully preserved papyri depicting ancient Egyptian life.

In addition to its rich historical offers, Turin incorporates modern art via sites such as Fondazione Sandretto Re Rebaudengo and Castello di Rivoli, where you can see new exhibits by Italian and international artists.

Aperitivo Culture

Turin is known for its strong aperitivo culture, which blends mingling with exquisite food and beverages. This ritual normally starts about 6 p.m., when establishments open their doors to serve a variety of beverages accompanied by appetizers.

One cannot visit Turin without enjoying a traditional Aperol Spritz or a glass of Vermouth di Torino, a fortified wine that originated in the city. For a genuine experience, visit Caffè Al Bicerin, where you can have their trademark drink, a wonderful blend of espresso, chocolate, and cream served in a glass.

For those searching for a vibrant environment, go to Piazza Vittorio Veneto, where various pubs flank the square and provide outdoor seating with spectacular views of the Po River and hills beyond. Here are some popular locations:

- **Bar Cavour** is well-known for its large vermouth range and masterfully constructed drinks.

- **Caffè San Carlo** is a classic café where you can people-watch while eating traditional delicacies.

- **Piazza San Carlo:** This attractive area is home to various pubs where people relax after work, making it a perfect place to experience true Turin life.

As you enjoy your aperitivo, don't forget to try some local favorites like tartufi (truffle-flavored appetizers) or salumi (cured meats), which are offered with your beverages.

Finally, Turin is an intriguing combination of regal history, cultural riches, and gastronomic pleasures, making it a must-see trip in Italy.

Whether you're visiting beautiful palaces or enjoying an aperitivo on a sun-drenched patio, this city provides amazing experiences at every turn. So take your camera and your appetite—Turin is waiting!

Lake Como

Lake Como, a gem in Northern Italy's crown, is a breathtakingly beautiful location that has enthralled travelers for ages. As I stepped on the beaches of this spectacular lake for the first time, I was stunned by the sheer majesty of the surrounding mountains, which reflected in the crystal-clear water. The aroma of lemon blossoms filled the air, and church bells echoed over the lowlands.

It was at that point that I fell in love with Lake Como, a passion that has only grown stronger with each subsequent visit.

Picturesque Lakeside Towns

Lake Como is filled with lovely villages, each with their distinct charms and attractions. Bellagio, sometimes known as the "Pearl of the Lake," is a real beauty. As you approach the town by boat, you'll be met with a breathtaking sight: **a** cluster of colorful buildings situated between two tree-covered promontories. The main center of Bellagio, Piazza della Chiesa, is the town's heart, surrounded by cafés, stores, and the majestic Basilica di San Giacomo. From here, you may stroll along the small, cobblestone alleys, taking in the beautiful houses and groomed gardens that border the beach.

Varenna, a lovely fishing hamlet, is just a short boat journey from Bellagio and has become a popular destination in its own right. Varenna's lovely promenade, the Passeggiata degli Innamorati (Lovers' Walk), provides breathtaking views of the lake and neighboring mountains. As you go down the lakeside, you will come across the Riva Grande, a little beach area ideal for sunbathing or swimming in the cold waters.

Don't miss out on visiting Villa Melzi, which is noted for its exquisite botanical gardens and art collection, or Villa Serbelloni, which has tiered grounds with panoramic lake views.

The town's historic center is a tangle of small streets and steep stairs leading to the Castello di Vezio, a medieval fortification with stunning panoramic views. Villa Monastero and Villa Cipressi are two of Varenna's most well-known attractions, featuring breathtaking gardens and museums that highlight the region's rich history and culture.

Other famous towns on Lake Como include Menaggio, which is noted for its busy promenade and golf course, and Tremezzo, which is home to the majestic Villa Carlotta and its renowned botanical gardens. Each town has its distinct personality and charm, making Lake Como an ideal destination for visitors looking for a blend of history, culture, and natural beauty.

Villas Balbianello and Carlotta

Lake Como is well-known for its exquisite homes, many of which are accessible to the public via tours and events. One of the most well-known is Villa del Balbianello, which is situated on a tiny peninsula near Lenno.

This 18th-century home was formerly held by Cardinal Angelo Maria Durini and then by the explorer Guido Monzino, who left it to the Fondo per l'Ambiente Italiano (FAI) after his death. Today, visitors may explore the villa's exquisite chambers, which include magnificent paintings, antique furniture, and a collection of Monzino's climbing mementos. The villa's grounds are a great showpiece, with tiered walks, elegant statuary, and stunning lake vistas.

Another must-see is Villa Carlotta, which is situated in Tremezzo. This 17th-century home was initially erected as a wedding present for Princess Marianne of Nassau and subsequently acquired by the Sommariva family.

Today, it is a museum with an excellent collection of art, including pieces by Canova, Thorvaldsen, and Hayez. The villa's grounds are similarly breathtaking, with lush flora, flowing waterfalls, and spectacular views of Lake Como and the neighboring mountains. Visitors may wander the grounds at their leisure or take a guided tour to learn about the villa's history and the flora that flourish in its environment.

Hiking and Boating Adventures (3.9.3)

Lake Como is an outdoor enthusiast's heaven, offering hiking and boating activities for all skill levels and interests. One of the most popular hiking paths is the Sentiero del Viandante (Wayfarer's Trail), which runs along the lake's eastern side from Abbadia Lariana to Piantedo.

This difficult trek provides breathtaking views of the lake and surrounding mountains, as well as the opportunity to visit attractive towns and historic buildings along the way. For those seeking a less challenging journey, the Greenway del Lago (Lake Greenway) is a 10-kilometer route that connects Colonno and Cadenabbia, going via the villages of Lenno, Mezzegra, and Tremezzo.

Lake Como is also a boater's dream, with several opportunities to explore the lake's various coves and inlets. You may hire a private boat, take a guided trip to see the lake's famed homes and gardens, or just sail about at your leisure.

Many villages along the lakeshore have boat rentals, ranging from tiny motorboats to bigger vessels that can accommodate parties of up to 12. For an unforgettable experience, schedule a sunset boat or a lakeside picnic replete with local specialties and superb Italian wines.

Lake Como will make a lasting impression, whether you are attracted to the region's spectacular natural beauty, rich history and culture, or dynamic outdoor lifestyle.

As you tour its quaint villages, gorgeous homes, and stunning scenery, you'll understand why this region of Northern Italy has caught the hearts and minds of travelers for generations. So pack your luggage, grab your camera, and prepare to start an incredible experience in one of Italy's most beautiful and popular places!

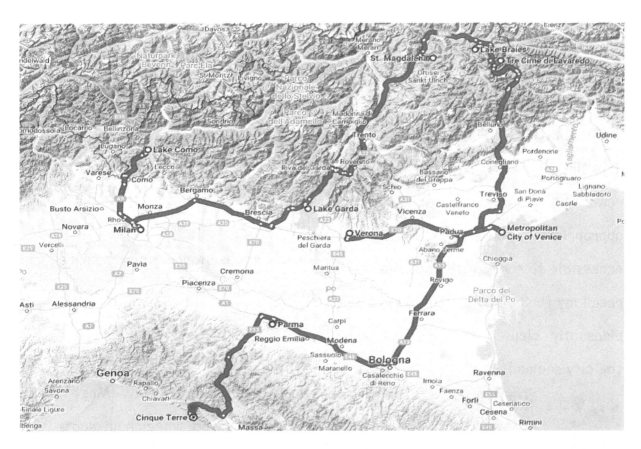

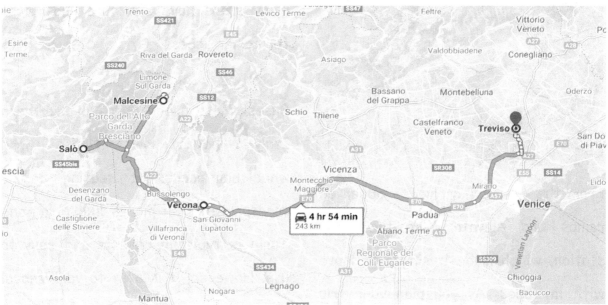

Chapter 4: Accessibility in Northern Italy.

Traveling With Disabilities

Traveling in Northern Italy may be a rewarding experience, and with the appropriate knowledge, it is also accessible to those with impairments. I recall my first visit to Milan when I was pleasantly pleased by how welcoming the city seemed.

From the minute I arrived, I observed ramps and elevators at the train station, which made it simple to move with my bags. As you plan your trip across Northern Italy, here's what you should know regarding accessible transportation and activities.

Transportation Options that Are Accessible

Trains: Italy has one of the greatest rail networks in Europe, with many stations outfitted with accessible amenities. The Sala Blu service assists travelers with impairments. You may ask for assistance while booking your ticket or by contacting them in advance. They will help you at the station and make sure you can board your train comfortably. Most trains have dedicated wheelchair spots, and many stops have elevators and ramps for easier access.

Buses: Most urban buses in Northern Italy have low floors and wheelchair-accessible seating. Public transportation in places like Milan and Turin is typically reliable and easy to use. However, it is best to verify local timetables since smaller towns may have limited bus service.

Taxis: Accessible taxis are available in large cities, however, they must often be reserved in advance. Many taxi firms provide wheelchair-accessible cars. Taxi2Airport and local taxi providers can assist you organize transportation.

Car Rentals: If you desire more freedom, try hiring a vehicle that meets your requirements. Some rental firms provide automobiles with hand controls and other adaptations.

Accessible Attractions

Many of Northern Italy's attractions are attempting to become more accessible.

Museums & Historical Sites: Most important museums, such as the Uffizi Gallery in Florence and the Egyptian Museum in Turin, include wheelchair access and personnel to help tourists.

Parks & Gardens: Many public parks, including Milan's Sempione Park and Lake Como's Villa Carlotta Gardens, feature wheelchair-accessible paved walkways.

Navigating Cities

Understanding the layouts of Northern Italian towns may substantially improve your experience. Many cities have pedestrian-friendly zones that are simpler to traverse.

Milan: The city center is largely level, with broad walkways. The famed retail area around Galleria Vittorio Emanuele II is accessible, with ramps connecting to stores and cafés. Public transportation is also well-connected, with convenient metro stations.

Venice: While Venice's canals provide unique problems owing to bridges and cobblestones, there are accessible Vaporetto (water bus) services that make it easy to get between islands. Some hotels also have accessible entrances.

Florence: The historic core is tiny and mainly pedestrianized, making it easy to explore on foot or in a wheelchair. Key sights, such as the Duomo, have accessible entrances.

Turin: With its broad boulevards and level terrain, Turin is easily accessible to persons with mobility issues. Public spaces, such as Piazza Castello, are vast and simple to explore.

Many cities provide information on accessible pathways via their tourism offices or websites. Don't be afraid to approach locals for help; Italians are famed for their generosity and eagerness to help.

Resources for Accessible Transportation

When traveling with a disability, proper planning is crucial. Here are some useful resources that **can help you:**

- **Sage Traveling:** This organization specializes in accessible travel in Italy and provides thorough information about numerous destinations, including suggestions for hotels, excursions, and transit alternatives designed specifically for disabled tourists.

- **Accessible Italian Holiday:** This website lists accessible lodgings and excursions of Northern Italy's lakes and towns. They provide bespoke packages that cater exclusively to those who want extra assistance.

- **Local Tourism Offices:** Every city has a tourism office where you may get maps of accessible routes and sights. For example, Florence's tourism bureau publishes a map of smoother streets that are good for wheelchairs.

- **Sala Blu Service at Trenitalia**: This service assists tourists with impairments in navigating train stations around Italy. The official Trenitalia website provides further information about their services.

By using these tools and preparing ahead of time, you may have a stress-free trip to Northern Italy. With its rich culture, breathtaking scenery, and inviting environment, this area offers something for everyone—regardless of mobility limitations! So pack your luggage with confidence; Northern Italy awaits your adventure!

Chapter 5: Experience Local Life in Northern Italy

Festivals and Celebration

Northern Italy is a lively fabric of culture and traditions, and its festivals reflect this rich legacy. During my travels, I had the opportunity to see some of these exciting events firsthand, each providing a unique peek into local life.

Carnevale di Venezia (Venice Carnival)

Venice turns into a glittering show each year during Carnevale, which takes place in February. This festival is known for its spectacular masks and costumes, and the festivities range from big balls to street plays.

The highlight is the Volo dell'Angelo, in which a performer disguised as an angel descends from the Campanile di San Marco to signal the formal start of the celebrations.

Try typical delights like as frittelle (fried doughnuts filled with cream) and chiacchiere (crispy pastries sprinkled with powdered sugar).

Festa del Redentore (Feast of the Redemption)

The Festa del Redentore takes place in mid-July in Venice to commemorate the end of a horrific epidemic in 1576. Locals assemble on boats in the lagoon to have picnics while watching a beautiful fireworks show illuminate the night sky. The atmosphere is electrifying as family and friends celebrate together—it's an excellent chance to sample Venetian hospitality.

Palio di Siena

This ancient horse race is held twice a year in Siena, on July 2 and August 16. The Palio is more than simply a marathon; it is a vivid festival of local culture, replete with parades of people costumed in medieval clothes representing several districts (contrade).

Each contrada battles hard for victory, and hundreds congregate in Piazza del Campo to support their horses. The atmosphere is vibrant, creating an amazing experience.

Festival of Madonna della Bruna

This celebration, held on July 2 in Matera, commemorates the town's patron saint with a magnificent parade led by a tall papier mâché monument. The event concludes with the spectacular burning of the monument, which represents regeneration and optimism.

The streets are alive with music, dancing, and superb local cuisine—a great opportunity to immerse yourself in Southern Italian culture. These festivals provide not only entertainment but also the chance to sample local cuisine and interact with the community. Each event represents the region's history and culture, making it a vital experience for every tourist.

Artisanal Crafts and Workshop

Northern Italy is known for its rich legacy of handcrafted crafts, and there are several possibilities to interact with local craftspeople via workshops and marketplaces.

Murano Glass Workshops

In Venice, you may visit Murano Island, which is famed for its excellent glassmaking. Many workshops provide hands-on opportunities to learn about the glassblowing process from professional artists. I spent an incredible day constructing my glass ornament with the help of an expert glassblower—it was both tough and gratifying!

Florentine Leather Workshops

Florence is recognized for producing high-quality leather items. Consider attending a session at a local leather school to discover methods utilized by craftspeople for years.

These workshops often involve crafting your leather items, such as a wallet or purse, so you may take home a one-of-a-kind keepsake created by your own hands.

Ceramics in Deruta.

Deruta, Umbria, is well-known for its magnificent pottery. Many studios provide classes where you may paint your ceramics using traditional methods. I spent the day painting tiles while drinking local wine—the ideal way to unwind and express your creativity!

Markets like Mercato Centrale in Florence and Piazza Navona in Rome are excellent locations to discover handcrafted products from local merchants. You may buy handcrafted items while supporting local craftspeople.

Immersive Culinary Experience

Food is central to Italian culture, and Northern Italy provides several options for immersive culinary experiences that enable visitors to learn about regional food firsthand.

Cooking Classes

Join a cooking lesson in Bologna, which is frequently regarded as Italy's gastronomic capital. Many sessions begin with a trip to a local market to pick out fresh ingredients before moving into the kitchen to learn how to cook classic meals like tagliatelle al ragù or tortellini from scratch.

I took part in one such session, which concluded with us eating our masterpieces over dinner coupled with superb local wines—an event I will never forget.

Food Tours

Consider joining a cuisine tour of places like Milan or Turin, where skilled guides will show you hidden treasures that offer traditional delicacies away from tourist traps. You'll have everything from street cuisine like arancini (fried rice balls) to regional delicacies like bagna cauda, all while learning about the history of each dish.

Wine Tasting Experiences

The wine districts around Lake Como and Tuscany provide excellent wine-sampling opportunities at local vineyards. Many vineyards provide guided tours that teach you about their winemaking processes, followed by tastings coupled with local cheeses and cured foods. During my visit to a winery near Chianti, I spent an afternoon admiring the gorgeous vistas of rolling hills while tasting great wines—an ideal experience.

Participating in local life via festivals, handcrafted crafts, and gastronomic experiences will enhance your trip across Northern Italy.

Each time spent immersed in these customs will leave you with lasting memories and a greater respect for this wonderful region's culture!

Chapter Six: Itineraries

Planning your vacation in Northern Italy can be an exciting experience, and having a well-structured schedule can help you make the most of your stay. Whether you have a weekend or two weeks, there is so much to discover! I recall my first vacation to Northern Italy when I methodically planned my days to make sure I didn't miss any of the breathtaking scenery, delectable cuisine, or colorful culture.

Here is a choice of itineraries to help you navigate this wonderful area.

Sample Itineraries for Various Durations.

If you just have a weekend in Milan, here's how **to maximize your time**:

Day One: Arrival and Exploration

- **Morning,** arrive in Milan and check into your hotel. Begin your day with a coffee and a pastry from Pasticceria Marchesi, one of Milan's classic pastry shops.
- **Late morning**: Visit the magnificent Duomo di Milano. Climb to the rooftop for stunning views of the city and a closer look at its ornate spires.
- **Afternoon**: Take a stroll around the Galleria Vittorio Emanuele II, where you may buy or just observe the beautiful architecture. Don't forget to spin the bull's testicles for good luck!
- **Evening**: Dine at Trattoria Milanese, where you may try classic delicacies such as risotto alla Milanese.

Day 2: Culture & Nightlife

- **Morning**: Go to Santa Maria delle Grazie to witness Leonardo da Vinci's The Last Supper. Make sure you reserve your tickets in advance!

- **Afternoon**: Visit Castello Sforzesco and the neighboring park, Parco Sempione. Take a stroll and have a picnic lunch.

- **Evening**: Go to the Navigli neighborhood for aperitivo. Visit Mag Cafè for drinks while seeing the bustling ambiance near the canals.

One Week Adventure: Exploring Venice and the Dolomites.

This program strikes a mix between Venice's romantic charm and the Dolomites' spectacular natural splendor.

Day One: Arrival in Venice.

- Arrive in Venice and check in to your hotel.

- Spend the day visiting St. Mark's Square and seeing St. Mark's Basilica.

Day Two: Venice Exploration

Take a gondola ride among the canals.

- Visit the Doge's Palace and visit the Rialto Market.

- Have supper in a classic Venetian osteria.

Day 3: Murano & Burano

- Take a boat to Murano and see glass blowing demonstrations.

- Continue to Burano, known for its colorful buildings and lace-making traditions.
- Return to Venice for an evening walk among the canals.

Day 4: Trip to the Dolomites

- Take an early train or bus to Bolzano, then transfer to your lodging in the Dolomites.
- Spend the day visiting Bolzano's picturesque old town.

Day 5: Hiking through the Dolomites

- Hike the Tre Cime di Lavaredo circuit, which offers breathtaking views of these legendary peaks.
- Return to your guesthouse for a sumptuous meal of local food.

Day 6: More Dolomite Adventures.

- Explore a different hiking track, such as Lago di Braies or Val Gardena.
- Consider hiring bicycles or participating in guided trips.

Day 7: Departure

- Return to Venice or Milan for your departure flight, allowing time for last-minute shopping or sightseeing.

Two Weeks: A Comprehensive Journey in Northern Italy

This tour takes you deep into Northern Italy's rich culture, history, and natural beauty.

Days 1-3: Milan

Follow the weekend schedule above, but add a day to spend visiting areas like Brera and Navigli during daytime hours.

Days 4-5: Lake Como

- Travel from Milan to Lake Como. Stay in Bellagio or Varenna.
- Spend two days seeing lovely villages, enjoying boat trips, and visiting homes such as Villa Carlotta.

Days 6-8: Venice

Head to Venice. Spend three days taking in the city's distinct atmosphere, seeing museums, and sampling local food.

Days 9-10: Verona and Bologna

- Travel to Verona (one hour by rail). Visit Juliet's House and experience this charming city.
- Continue to Bologna (1 hour by rail) for two days of gastronomic treats and historical attractions.

Days 11-12: The Dolomites

- Head to the Dolomites for trekking activities. Spend two days hiking trails and sampling local mountain food.

Days 13-14: Turin and departure

- End your tour in Turin, where you may explore royal homes and enjoy aperitivo culture before returning home.

Customizable Itinerary Tips

Tailoring your schedule around your unique interests may considerably improve your trip experience. Here are a few tips:

Art Lovers:

Concentrate on places recognized for their art scenes, such as Florence and Milan. Include trips to galleries like the Uffizi Gallery and the Pinacoteca di Brera.

Food enthusiasts:

Incorporate culinary courses in Bologna or food excursions in Turin that focus on local specialties such as pasta-making or cheese sampling.

Outdoor adventurers:

If hiking is your passion, consider visiting places like the Dolomites or Lake Como, where you can discover picturesque routes and appreciate nature.

Cultural immersion:

Attend local festivals that coincide with your vacation dates; they provide unique insights into area culture and food.

Flexibility is key.

Allow some time in each place for unplanned discoveries, such as visiting a quiet café or stumbling upon a local market! Customizing your schedule based on what fascinates you the most about Northern Italy will result in an amazing tour packed with experiences that are intimately relevant to your interests. So pack your luggage with enthusiasm—Northern Italy is waiting to greet you!

Chapter 7: Practical Information.

As you plan your trip to Northern Italy, it's crucial to grasp the visa and entrance procedures, acquaint yourself with transportation alternatives, and learn some basic Italian words. While these issues may not be the most exciting aspects of travel preparation, they are critical to having a pleasant and hassle-free journey.

I recall my first trip to Italy when I had to manage the rail system and speak with folks who spoke little English. Having a rudimentary awareness of these practical things improved my capacity to fully enjoy the vacation.

Visa and Entry Requirements.

Italy is a signatory to the Schengen Agreement, which provides for free movement between participating nations. Depending on your nationality, you may need a visa to enter Italy.

Here is a brief overview:

EU nationals may enter Italy with a valid national ID card or passport and do not need a visa.

- Citizens of the United States, Canada, Australia, and New Zealand are permitted to visit Italy without a visa for up to 90 days for tourism or business. Your passport must be valid for at least three months after your scheduled visit.

- **Other nationalities**: Travelers from other nations may be required to get a Schengen visa before entering Italy. The visa application procedure might take many weeks, so apply well ahead of your trip. Requirements differ by country of origin, so contact your local Italian embassy or consulate for precise details.

Regardless of your country, it's always a good idea to have a valid passport with you while visiting Italy. Some attractions may also demand a valid ID to enter, so keep your passport and a photocopy of it with you at all times.

Transportation Tips

Northern Italy's well-developed transportation network makes it relatively simple to get about. Here are some pointers to navigate the system:

Trains:

Trenitalia and Italo run Italy's high-speed rail network, which links the majority of northern Italy's main cities.

Tickets may be bought online, at rail stations, or from approved stores. Prices vary according to the type of service and time of travel but expect to spend between €50 and €100 for a one-way ticket between major cities.

If you want to travel long distances by train, consider obtaining a Eurail or Italy Rail Pass. These passes provide substantial savings and flexibility.

Download the Trenitalia app or go to the Trenitalia website to check timetables and buy tickets in advance.

Buses:

- Various firms, including SITA and Autostradale, run regional and intercity buses.
- Tickets may be bought from approved vendors, such as tobacco stores (tabacchi) or at the bus terminal.
- Prices vary based on distance and business but expect to spend between €10 and €30 for a one-way ticket.

Taxis:

Taxis are easily accessible in big cities, and they may be hailed on the street or located at authorized taxi stops.

Fares are metered and range from €3 to €5 for the first boarding cost, plus an extra €1 to €2 for each kilometer.

Avoid using taxis from tourist areas, since they may charge more. Instead, contact your hotel or a local for a suggested cab service.

Ferries:

- Ferries are a popular method to visit the Italian Lakes and the Ligurian coast.
- Services connect major towns and cities, with costs changing according to distance and ticket type (one-way or round-trip).
- Reservations are essential, particularly during high season. Tickets may be purchased online or at the ferry station.

Useful Italian Phrases

Learning a few key Italian words will help you manage your vacation and interact with locals. Here are 20 useful phrases:

1. Hello - Ciao (CHOW)
2. Good morning - Buongiorno (BWON-jor-no)
3. Good evening - Buonasera (BWON-ah-seh-rah)
4. Please - Per favore (PER fah-voh-reh)
5. Thank you - Grazie (GRAH-tsee-eh)
6. You're welcome - Prego (PREH-goh)
7. Excuse me - Scusi (SKOO-zee)
8. I'm sorry - Mi dispiace (mee dees-pya-cheh)

9. Do you speak English? - Parla inglese? (PAR-lah een-gleh-zeh?)

10. I don't understand - Non capisco (non kah-pee-sko)

11. Where is...? - Dov'è...? (doh-VEH?)

12. How much is it? - Quanto costa? (KWAN-toh KAW-stah?)

13. I would like... - Vorrei... (vohr-RAY...)

14. The bill, please - Il conto, per favore (eel KON-toh, pehr fah-voh-reh)

15. Yes - Sì (see)

16. No - No (noh)

17. Cheers! - Salute! (sah-LOO-teh!)

18. Delicious - Buonissimo (bwoh-nee-see-moh)

19. Beautiful - Bellissimo (bel-lee-see-moh)

20. Goodbye - Arrivederci (ah-ree-veh-DEHR-chee)

Remember, Italians love it when foreigners try to speak their language, even if it's just a few simple words. Don't be scared to practice and interact with locals; they'll probably be delighted to assist you improve your Italian! You'll be well-prepared to confidently travel to Northern Italy if you're acquainted with visa procedures, transportation alternatives, and key Italian words. These practical things may not be the most exciting aspects of your vacation preparation, but they will allow you to appreciate the gorgeous scenery, rich history, and great food that make this area so unique. So plunge in, learn a few basic words, and prepare for an incredible journey around Northern Italy!

Conclusion

As I ponder on my fantastic adventure to Northern Italy, I am overwhelmed with awe and thankfulness. This area has made an unforgettable impression on my heart, from the beautiful scenery of the Dolomites to Venice's quaint canals, and all in between. One of my favorite memories is stumbling onto a secret trattoria in Bologna and eating the most wonderful tagliatelle al ragù of my life.

The proprietor, Gianni, a devoted local, greeted me like family and requested I eat his handmade tiramisu. As I sat there, surrounded by the friendly banter of locals, I realized I'd encountered the genuine core of Northern Italian friendliness.

Another memorable experience was viewing the sunset over Lake Como from the grounds of Villa del Balbianello.

The golden light swirled over the river, highlighting the colorful homes along the beach. It was a sight right out of a dream, and I felt fortunate to see such natural beauty.

But probably the most powerful effect of my visits was the feeling of history that pervades every area of Northern Italy. From the Roman remains of Turin to the Renaissance masterpieces of Florence, I was continually reminded of this region's lasting heritage. Tracing the footsteps of great artists and intellectuals helped me feel linked to something bigger than myself.

As I prepare to say goodbye to Northern Italy, I know that I will return home permanently altered. This travel has instilled a greater appreciation for life's little pleasures—a well-brewed cappuccino, a walk around a centuries-old piazza, or a talk with an enthusiastic local. These are the moments that make travel so life-changing and uplifting.

So, to my fellow travelers, I say arrivederci, not farewell. Northern Italy is a region that begs to be returned over and again. Its attraction is everlasting, and its charm is compelling. May this book serve as a springboard for your own wonderful experience in this extraordinary part of the globe. Have a good trip!

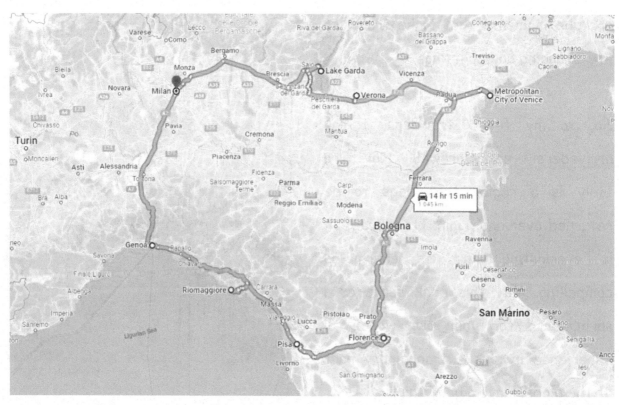

Made in the USA
Las Vegas, NV
24 December 2024

15329949R00044